Who We Are

Published by
MNM Publishing

ISBN-13: 978-1-7371946-0-6

Book Cover and Interior Design:
Jessica Tilles of TWA Solutions

Who We Are

Michael Timmons

TABLE OF CONTENTS

HOW AFRICA GOT ITS NAME

Africa got its name after Scipio defeated Hannibal of Carthage in the Second Punic War. Carthage being a state that existed around modern-day Tunisia, he became known as Scipio Africanus, or Scipio the African, as a way of honoring him for his victory in Africa.

Before Africa, the Kemetic or Alkebu-Ian history of Afrika suggests that the ancient name of the continent was Alkebulan. The word Alkebu-Ian is the oldest and the only word of indigenous origin. Alkebulan meaning the garden of Eden or the mother of mankind. In the Bible, Libya is the word used for the continent. For the sake of this book, we will refer to the continent as Africa.

NEGROLAND

*T*he first Black slaves were from West Africa (the slave coast) and transported to the English colonies in America in 1619. Believe it or not, it wasn't by coincidence they were the chosen people. I intend to show you the evidence in this book that the God of Abraham, Isaac, and Jacob has allowed His chosen people to suffer because of their disobedience and also how His people will be identified by their sufferings. I will show you whom and how they stole their identity.

A new and accurate map of Africa was drawn by the best and most approved Modern Maps and Charts and regulated by Astronomical Observations by Emanual Bowen from the year 1747. I stumbled upon this map a few years ago and I believe things don't happen by chance, so I believe it was destined for me to find this information to share it with others. On this map, just above Guinea, was a place called Negroland.

The transatlantic slave trade took Blacks from Negroland to the four corners of the Earth. Blacks taken to North America, including the Caribbean, left mainly from West Africa. Enslaved Blacks were imported into the Caribbean and South America, with about six percent were sent to the British colonies in North America. There were approximately twelve and a half million Blacks taken during that transatlantic slave trade, but what many don't know or refuse to acknowledge is that the East African slave trade took over seventeen million Blacks to the Middle East, India, and North Africa. The latter we will discuss in another book.

It always baffled me why Africans sold their people to slave traders. Well, that was before I learned that every person with dark skin living on the African continent was not African. Unbelievable! Now, this raised other questions such as, who were these other people of color that were living there and where did they come from? I learned as a child and always just assumed that all people with dark skin were descendants of Noah's son, Ham. I was about to discover just how wrong my teachings were.

Most of the slaves taken from Africa during the trans-Atlantic slave trade came from Negroland and were targets, and it was not an accident. It has been historically proven that these people were descendants of early Hebrews that migrated from Jerusalem, Egypt, and Ethiopia into West Africa. Native African tribes and Muslims attacked these people sold them to European slave traders who then transported them to North, South, and Central America.

The Kingdom of Widah or also known as Judea was a kingdom on the coast of West Africa in what is now Benin. It was a major slave trading area. In Creole New Orleans Race and Americanization by Arnold R. Hirsch and Joseph Logsdon, there are notes written by a trader that reads: Six ships came from Juda and landed at the mouth of the Mississippi and in 1731 one ship from Juda landed four hundred and sixty-four slaves at the mouth of the Mississippi. On page sixty-nine in the chapter titled "The Formation of Afro-Creole Culture," there is a chart listing the origin and number of slaves brought to Louisiana. Between 1719 and 1728, there were one thousand seven hundred forty-nine Blacks taken from Judah (Whydah).

The Kingdom of Whydah (also spelled Hueda, Whidah, Ajuda, Ouidah, Whidaw, Juida, and Juda) was a kingdom on the coast of West Africa in what is now Benin. It was a major slave trading area. In 1700, it had a coastline of around ten miles. Under King Haffon, it expanded to forty miles and stretched twenty-five miles inland. Juda is Judah, one of the twelve tribes of Israel. There was a diaspora of the Israelites which started in 597 B.C when Nebuchadnezzar II, king of Babylon invaded and defeated Judah. Some fled to Egypt but most ended up on the west coast of Africa and through slavery were scattered to the four corners of the world.

Centered in Savi, the last ruler of the Kingdom of Whydah was King Haffon, who was deposed in 1727 when the Kingdom of Dahomey conquered (and annexed) Whydah.

Labeled on the map of Africa from 1747 was the grain coast, which was obviously where they acquired grain. From the tooth coast and the gold coast, they acquired gold and ivory. Next to the gold coast was the slave coast. This map led the slave traders right to Juda (Whydah), Negroland.

Why is this important? According to the Bible, the twelve tribes of Israel were split into two kingdoms. The southern kingdom only comprised the tribes of Judah and Benjamin and thus became the kingdom of Judah, with Jerusalem being its capital.

This map was created in 1747 by English cartographer, Emmanuel Bowen, as part of a collection. He was a renowned map maker with a reputation for being accurate. On this map of Negroland (Africa), he noted, "The Kingdom of Juda" as "The Slave Coast."

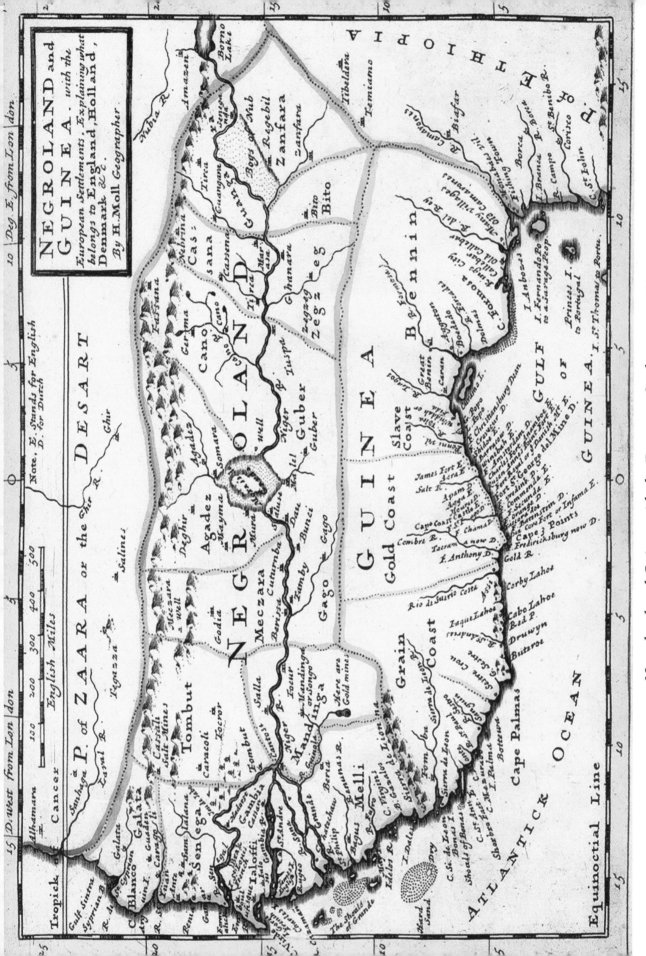

Negroland and Guinea with the European Settlements, 1736.

WHY WERE THESE
PEOPLE TAKEN?

The following Bible verses below are taken from Deuteronomy 28:41-68, where God let us know we will identify His people.

⁴¹You shall beget sons and daughters, but they shall not be yours; for they shall go into captivity. 42 Locusts shall consume all your trees and the produce of your land.

⁴³The alien who is among you shall rise higher and higher above you, and you shall come down lower and lower.

⁴⁴He shall lend to you, but you shall not lend to him; he shall be the head, and you shall be the tail.

45 Moreover all these curses shall come upon you and pursue and overtake you, until you are destroyed, because you did not obey the voice of the Lord your God, to keep His commandments and His statutes which He commanded you.

46 And they shall be upon you for a sign and a wonder, and on your descendants forever.

47 "Because you did not serve the Lord your God with joy and gladness of heart, for the abundance of everything, 48 therefore you shall serve your enemies, whom the Lord will send against you, in hunger, in thirst, in nakedness, and in need of everything; and He will put a yoke of iron on your neck until He has destroyed you.

⁴⁹The Lord will bring a nation against you from afar, from the end of the earth, as swift as the eagle flies, a nation whose language you will not understand,

⁵⁰a nation of fierce countenance, which does not respect the elderly nor show favor to the young.

⁵¹And they shall eat the increase of your livestock and the produce of your land, until you are destroyed; they shall not leave you grain or new wine or oil, or the increase of your cattle or the offspring of your flocks, until they have destroyed you.

⁵²They shall besiege you at all your gates until your high and fortified walls, in which you trust, come down throughout all your land; and they shall besiege you at all your gates throughout all your land which the Lord your God has given you.

⁵³ You shall eat the fruit of your own body, the flesh of your sons and your daughters whom the Lord your God has given you, in the siege and desperate straits in which your enemy shall distress you.

⁵⁴The sensitive and very refined man among you will be hostile toward his brother, toward the wife of his bosom, and toward the rest of his children whom he leaves behind, ⁵⁵so that he will not give any of them the flesh of his children whom he will eat, because he has nothing left in the siege and desperate straits in which your enemy shall distress you at all your gates. ⁵⁶ The tender and delicate woman among you, who would not venture to set the sole of her foot on the ground because of her delicateness and sensitivity, will refuse to the husband of her bosom, and to her son and her daughter, ⁵⁷ her placenta which comes out from between her feet and her children whom she bears; for she will eat them secretly for lack of everything in the siege and desperate straits in which your enemy shall distress you at all your gates.

⁵⁸ "If you do not carefully observe all the words of this law that are written in this book, that you may fear this glorious and awesome name, THE LORD YOUR GOD,

⁵⁹ then the Lord will bring upon you and your descendants extraordinary plagues—great and prolonged plagues—and serious and prolonged sicknesses.

⁶⁰ Moreover He will bring back on you all the diseases of Egypt, of which you were afraid, and they shall cling to you.

61 Also every sickness and every plague, which is not written in this Book of the Law, will the Lord bring upon you until you are destroyed.

62 You shall be left few in number, whereas you were as the stars of heaven in multitude, because you would not obey the voice of the Lord your God.

63 And it shall be, that just as the Lord rejoiced over you to do you good and multiply you, so the Lord will rejoice over you to destroy you and bring you to nothing; and you shall be plucked from off the land which you go to possess.

64 "Then the Lord will scatter you among all peoples, from one end of the earth to the other, and there you shall serve other gods, which neither you nor your fathers have known—wood and stone.

65 And among those nations you shall find no rest, nor shall the sole of your foot have a resting place; but there the Lord will give you a trembling heart, failing eyes, and anguish of soul.

66 Your life shall hang in doubt before you; you shall fear day and night, and have no assurance of life.

67 In the morning you shall say, 'Oh, that it were evening!' And at evening you shall say, 'Oh, that it were morning!' because of the fear which terrifies your heart, and because of the sight which your eyes see.

68 And the Lord will take you back to Egypt in ships, by the way of which I said to you, 'You shall never see it again.' And there you shall be offered for sale to your enemies as male and female slaves, but no one will buy you."

God's chosen people will be identified by the curses in Deuteronomy 28! You tell me what group of people was taken to a foreign land by ship and bought and sold into slavery? What group of people was scattered from one end of the Earth to the other? "The Lord will take you back into Egypt by ships."

In Washington, DC, the IKG Cultural Resource Center does a tour called "Egypt on the Potomac" and this is what they show you: "Nile Valley culture lives in the monuments of the

District of Columbia. You will see evidence of ancient Egyptian architecture, symbolism, and philosophy that has been embedded in various monuments throughout the city…literally hidden in plain sight. You will understand how the shape, orientation, and location of the District of Columbia reveals a plan crafted by America's founding fathers, designed to recreate the spiritual essence of Egypt along the Potomac." This is more evidence, proving Deuteronomy 28.

So how and what does this verse have to do with Negroland and the people who lived there? For the answer to those questions, we have to travel back in time to get a clearer picture.

Zondervan's Pictorial Bible Dictionary describes Ham as, "The youngest son of Noah, born probably about 96 years before the flood; and one of the eight persons to live through the flood. He became the progenitor of the dark races; not the Negroes, but the Egyptians, Libyans, and the Canaanites." I have always heard pastors preach that all Blacks are descendants of Noah's son, Ham. Obviously, after reading this, I had to dig much deeper to get the truth. So I started with the lineage of another one of Noah's sons, Shem, and this is what I discovered.

Shem had five sons: Elam, Asshur, Arphaxad, Lud, and Aram. For the sake of this book, we will follow Arphaxad through time. In the past, when reading the scriptures, I skimmed over the readings of the lineages because I didn't think they had any meaning or relevance to us today. I was about to discover how wrong I was and how important they are. When you research on your own, which I sincerely urge you to do, the Table of Nations will be the cornerstone of your research. In Genesis 11, there is the lineage of Shem:

"These are the generations of Shem: Shem was a hundred years old and begat Arphaxad two years after the flood:

[11]And Shem lived after he begat Arphaxad five hundred years, and begat sons and daughters.

[12]And Arphaxad lived five and thirty years, and begat Salah:

[13]And Arphaxad lived after he begat Salah four hundred and three years, and begat sons and daughters.

¹⁴And Salah lived thirty years, and begat Eber:

¹⁵And Salah lived after he begat Eber four hundred and three years, and begat sons and daughters.

¹⁶And Eber lived four and thirty years, and begat Peleg:

¹⁷And Eber lived after he begat Peleg four hundred and thirty years, and begat sons and daughters.

¹⁸And Peleg lived thirty years, and begat Reu:

¹⁹And Peleg lived after he begat Reu two hundred and nine years, and begat sons and daughters.

²⁰And Reu lived two and thirty years, and begat Serug:

²¹And Reu lived after he begat Serug two hundred and seven years, and begat sons and daughters.

²²And Serug lived thirty years, and begat Nahor:

²³And Serug lived after he begat Nahor two hundred years, and begat sons and daughters.

²⁴And Nahor lived nine and twenty years, and begat Terah:

²⁵And Nahor lived after he begat Terah a hundred and nineteen years, and begat sons and daughters.

²⁶And Terah lived seventy years, and begat Abram, Nahor, and Haran.

²⁷Now these are the generations of Terah: Terah begat Abram, Nahor, and Haran; and Haran begat Lot.

Terah was the father of Abram and the grandfather to Lot. Terah's son, Abram, had an encounter with God who told him to leave Ur of Mesopotamia, which was part of Sumer to go to the land of Canaan. This account takes place in Genesis 11:28. So, before I go further, let me go over a few things.

Arphaxad was the father of Shelah who was the father of Eber who had two sons that were born to him. Numbers 24:24 says the children of Eber, and though he had other children because he was their father not only by natural generation but also regarding the promise of God, was conveyed to them through Shem's hands.

One was named Peleg because in his days on the Earth was divided, and his brother was named Joktan. Peleg means division. One belief is that Pangea, also spelled Pangaea, in early geologic times there was a supercontinent that incorporated almost all the landmasses on Earth. Some believe that the Bible, during the days of Peleg, it is describing the division of the continents. His name could also refer to the account in the Bible when the whole Earth was of one language and one speech when the people tried to build a tower to the heavens and God caused them to speak different languages. The name of it became known as the Tower of Babel because God confused the language of all the Earth and scattered them abroad upon the face of all the Earth.

Born in a time of turmoil, Reu (whose name means "pasture" or "friend") was part of the tribe of Shem, who had a son two years after the Great Flood. His family stayed in Ur after the dispersion of the tribes from Babel. Serug was Abraham's great-great-grandfather.

Genesis Chapter 11, lists Nahor (not to be confused with Nahor II) as the son of Serug. He was also the grandfather of Abraham, Nahor II, and Haran, all descendants of Shem.

Terah was the father of Abram, later called Abraham. It was Terah's son, Abram, with whom God established a covenant to bless all the families of the Earth. According to Genesis 11:31, And Terah took Abram his son, and Lot the son of Haran his son's son, and Sarai his daughter in law, his son Abram's wife; and they went forth with them from Ur of the Chaldees, to go into the land of Canaan; and they came to Haran, and dwelled there.

The biography.yourdictionary.com says, "Abraham was born Abram, son of Terah, at the beginning of the second millennium BC in Ur, the capital of Mesopotamia at the height of its splendor as a highly developed ancient world. According to Jewish tradition, he was the son of an idol maker and smashed all of his father's idols—except one—in a story that foreshadows his devotion to one God."

An interesting story is found in Jasher 8:

1 "And it was in the night that Abram was born, that all the servants of Terah, and all the wise men of Nimrod, and his conjurors came and ate and drank in the house of Terah, and they rejoiced with him on that night.

2 And when all the wise men and conjurors went out from the house of Terah, they lifted up their eyes toward heaven that night to look at the stars, and they saw, and behold one very large star came from the east and ran in the heavens, and he swallowed up the four stars from the four sides of the heavens.

3 And all the wise men of the king and his conjurors were astonished at the sight, and the sages understood this matter, and they knew its import.

4 And they said to each other, This only betokens the child that has been born to Terah this night, who will grow up and be fruitful, and multiply, and possess all the earth, he and his children for ever, and he and his seed will slay great kings, and inherit their lands.

5 And the wise men and conjurors went home that night, and in the morning all these wise men and conjurors rose up early, and assembled in an appointed house.

6 And they spoke and said to each other, Behold the sight that we saw last night is hidden from the king, it has not been made known to him.

7 And should this thing get known to the king in the latter days, he will say to us, Why have you concealed this matter from me, and then we shall all suffer death; therefore, now let us go and tell the king the sight which we saw, and the interpretation thereof, and we shall then remain clear.

8 And they did so, and they all went to the king and bowed down to him to the ground, and they said, May the king live, may the king live.

9 We heard that a son was born to Terah the son of Nahor, the prince of thy host, and we yesternight came to his house, and we ate and drank and rejoiced with him that night.

10 And when thy servants went out from the house of Terah, to go to our respective homes to abide there for the night, we lifted up our eyes to heaven, and we saw a great star coming from the east, and the same star ran with great speed, and swallowed up four great stars, from the four sides of the heavens.

¹¹ And thy servants were astonished at the sight which we saw, and were greatly terrified, and we made our judgment upon the sight, and knew by our wisdom the proper interpretation thereof, that this thing applies to the child that is born to Terah, who will grow up and multiply greatly, and become powerful, and kill all the kings of the earth, and inherit all their lands, he and his seed forever.

¹² And now our lord and king, behold we have truly acquainted thee with what we have seen concerning this child.

¹³ If it seemeth good to the king to give his father value for this child, we will slay him before he shall grow up and increase in the land, and his evil increase against us, that we and our children perish through his evil.

¹⁴ And the king heard their words and they seemed good in his sight, and he sent and called for Terah, and Terah came before the king.

¹⁵ And the king said to Terah, I have been told that a son was yesternight born to thee, and after this manner was observed in the heavens at his birth.

¹⁶ And now therefore give me the child, that we may slay him before his evil springs up against us, and I will give thee for his value, thy house full of silver and gold.

¹⁷ And Terah answered the king and said to him: My Lord and king, I have heard thy words, and thy servant shall do all that his king desireth.

¹⁸ But my lord and king, I will tell thee what happened to me yesternight, that I may see what advice the king will give his servant, and then I will answer the king upon what he has just spoken; and the king said, Speak.

¹⁹ And Terah said to the king, Ayon, son of Mored, came to me yesternight, saying,

²⁰ Give unto me the great and beautiful horse that the king gave thee, and I will give thee silver and gold, and straw and provender for its value; and I said to him, Wait till I see the king concerning thy words, and behold whatever the king saith, that will I do.

²¹ And now my lord and king, behold I have made this thing known to thee, and the advice which my king will give unto his servant, that will I follow.

²² *And the king heard the words of Terah, and his anger was kindled and he considered him in the light of a fool.*

²³ *And the king answered Terah, and he said to him, Art thou so silly, ignorant, or deficient in understanding, to do this thing, to give thy beautiful horse for silver and gold or even for straw and provender?*

²⁴ *Art thou so short of silver and gold, that thou shouldst do this thing, because thou canst not obtain straw and provender to feed thy horse? and what is silver and gold to thee, or straw and provender, that thou shouldst give away that fine horse which I gave thee, like which there is none to be had on the whole earth?*

²⁵ *And the king left off speaking, and Terah answered the king, saying, Like unto this has the king spoken to his servant;*

²⁶ *I beseech thee, my lord and king, what is this which thou didst say unto me, saying, Give thy son that we may slay him, and I will give thee silver and gold for his value; what shall I do with silver and gold after the death of my son? who shall inherit me? surely then at my death, the silver and gold will return to my king who gave it.*

²⁷ *And when the king heard the words of Terah, and the parable which he brought concerning the king, it grieved him greatly and he was vexed at this thing, and his anger burned within him.*

²⁸ *And Terah saw that the anger of the king was kindled against him, and he answered the king, saying, All that I have is in the king's power; whatever the king desireth to do to his servant, that let him do, yea, even my son, he is in the king's power, without value in exchange, he and his two brothers that are older than he.*

²⁹ *And the king said to Terah, No, but I will purchase thy younger son for a price.*

³⁰ *And Terah answered the king, saying, I beseech thee my lord and king to let thy servant speak a word before thee, and let the king hear the word of his servant, and Terah said, Let my king give me three days' time till I consider this matter within myself, and consult with my family concerning the words of my king; and he pressed the king greatly to agree to this.*

³¹ And the king hearkened to Terah, and he did so and he gave him three days' time, and Terah went out from the king's presence, and he came home to his family and spoke to them all the words of the king; and the people were greatly afraid.

³² And it was in the third day that the king sent to Terah, saying, Send me thy son for a price as I spoke to thee; and shouldst thou not do this, I will send and slay all thou hast in thy house, so that thou shalt not even have a dog remaining.

³³ And Terah hastened, (as the thing was urgent from the king), and he took a child from one of his servants, which his handmaid had born to him that day, and Terah brought the child to the king and received value for him.

³⁴ And the Lord was with Terah in this matter, that Nimrod might not cause Abram's death, and the king took the child from Terah and with all his might dashed his head to the ground, for he thought it had been Abram; and this was concealed from him from that day, and it was forgotten by the king, as it was the will of Providence not to suffer Abram's death.

³⁵ And Terah took Abram his son secretly, together with his mother and nurse, and he concealed them in a cave, and he brought them their provisions monthly.

³⁶ And the Lord was with Abram in the cave and he grew up, and Abram was in the cave ten years, and the king and his princes, soothsayers and sages, thought that the king had killed Abram."

Two generations later Abraham's grandson Esau came upon Nimrod in the field alone and saw this as his opportunity to kill him. Esau attacked Nimrod and did kill him. He cried out for help but by the time his men arrived it was too late, Esau had already killed Nimrod and stolen his special garments. It was after this altercation with Nimrod that Esau returned home exhausted and hungry and sold his birthright.

Abram lived in the house of Noah until the age of fifty before going to live in the house of his father. Being raised in the house of Noah, Abram knew the ways and instruction of the true God. During this time, Nimrod was still ruling Babylon and worshiping many false gods. Terah (Abram's father) was the captain of the host of King Nimrod and he as well worshipped many false gods. The book of Jasher tells of a time when Abram confronts his father about his idol worship and King Nimrod of Babylon condemned him to burn in a furnace, but God protected him. Later, King Nimrod, at the advice of his wise men, decided he would have Abram killed. Abram, hearing this, hid in the house of Noah and Shem. It was after this that Abram and his family left Ur—in modern-day Iraq—to travel northwest along the trade route and the Euphrates River to the city of Haran. Abram settled down in Haran—in modern-day Israel—with his family. He married Sarai and entered a lifelong partnership with her. Haran—as well as all the neighboring cities and countries—was a land devoted to polytheism.

In Genesis 12:1-7, the Lord had said to Abram: *"Get out of your country, From your family and from your father's house, To a land that I will show you*

2 I will make you a great nation; I will bless you And make your name great; And you shall be a blessing

3 I will bless those who bless you, And I will curse him who curses you;

And in you all the families of the earth shall be blessed."

4 So Abram departed as the Lord had spoken to him, and Lot went with him. And Abram was seventy-five years old when he departed from Haran.

5 Then Abram took Sarai his wife and Lot his brother's son, and all their possessions that they had gathered, and the people whom they had acquired in Haran, and they departed to go to the land of Canaan. So they came to the land of Canaan.

6 Abram passed through the land to the place of Shechem, as far as the terebinth tree of Moreh. And the Canaanites were then in the land.

7 Then the Lord appeared to Abram and said, "To your descendants I will give this land." And there he built an altar to the Lord, who had appeared to him.

Ur was a major Sumerian city-state in Mesopotamia, marked today by Tell el-Muqayyar in southern Iraq.

Sumer was an ancient civilization founded in the Mesopotamia region of the Fertile Crescent, situated between the Tigris and Euphrates rivers. Known for their innovations in language, governance, architecture, and more, Sumerians are considered the creators of civilization.

In 1933, the Mari tablets were discovered in the ancient Sumerian and Canaan cities in Syria, which describes the Sumerian people as the Black-headed people or Black-headed ones.

In the Sumerian period, Susa was the capital of a state called Susiana. Control of Susiana shifted between Elam, Sumer, and Akkad. Susiana is sometimes mistaken as synonymous with Elam but, according to F. Vallat, it was a distinct cultural and political entity. During the Elamite monarch, many riches and materials were brought to Susa from the destruction of other cities. This was because of Susa's location to the city of Babylon and other cities in Mesopotamia. Remember, Elam was one of the five sons of Shem. Daniel had a vision, which is written in the Daniel 8:2, "I looked in the vision, and while I was looking I was in the citadel of Susa, which is in the province of Elam; and I looked in the vision and I myself was beside the Ulai Canal."

On the next page is a picture that is on the wall inside the Palace of Darius in Susa.

So Abraham, the father of Isaac who was the father of Esau and Jacob, lived in the land of Sumer. They not only described themselves as Black-headed people but according to the drawings on the walls, they also drew themselves as being blacks in color.

After Abraham died, in Genesis 26:3-5, God repeated and reinforced the promises to Abraham's son, Isaac, and his grandson, Jacob. God told Isaac, "Dwell in this land, and I will be with you and bless you; for to you and your descendants I give all these lands, and I will perform the oath which I swore to Abraham your father. And I will make your descendants multiply as the stars of heaven; I will give to your descendants all these lands; and in your seed all the nations of the earth shall be blessed; because Abraham obeyed My voice and kept My charge, My commandments, My statutes, and My laws."

This is where the story gets really interesting. Abraham had a son by the name of Isaac. The Bible tells the story of Isaac and his wife, Rebekah. Rebekah became pregnant with twins and they struggled inside of her. It was so bad that she thought, If it's going to be like

this, I'm not so sure I even want to be pregnant. Now imagine how bad this must have been because she was childless before this and Isaac had prayed to God for her to become pregnant. Rebekah finally prayed to God, and He told her, "Two nations are in your womb, and two peoples will be separated from within you. One people will be stronger than the other and the older will serve the younger."

Those twins that struggled in the womb of their mother were Esau and Jacob. When the brothers were older, with Esau being the oldest, he received the birthright and the blessing as the firstborn. Esau sold his birthright to his brother, Jacob. Jacob would later deceive their father into giving him the blessing that was traditionally for the firstborn. These brothers would become nations and just as God told Rebekah, "Two nations are war in your womb," Esau hated his brother, Jacob. Esau's offspring would be known as the Edomites and Jacob's name would be changed to Israel and his offspring would be known as the Israelites. From that time on, the Edomites would be the enemy of the Israelites and would eventuality deceive the world into believing they were the chosen people, that they are the Israelites.

Those familiar with the Bible know that God changed the name of Jacob to Israel.

Below are the twelve sons of Jacob (Israel) and the meaning of their names:

- Reuben – Behold, a son is born to us
- Simeon – One who hears
- Levi – Attached
- Judah – Praise the Lord
- Dan – He judged
- Naphtali – My struggle
- Gad – Good fortune
- Asher – Happiness
- Issachar – Reward
- Zebulun – Honour

- Joseph – Add to my family
- Benjamin – Son of righteousness

As we know, the twelve sons of Jacob (Israel) became the twelve tribes of Israel. Israel comprised twelve tribes until ten of the twelve tribes of Israel were said to have been deported from the Kingdom of Israel. It is written (1 Kings 11:26-43; 12: 1-33; 14: 21-31) that after King Solomon died, Jeroboam became king of these ten tribes. King Jeroboam did not want his people to go to Jerusalem to worship at the temple, so he made two golden calves for his people to worship. The ten tribes of Israel in the North under King Jeroboam were disobedient, so God allowed them to be conquered by the Neo-Assyrian Empire in about 722 BCE. These were the tribes of Reuben, Simeon, Dan, Naphtali, Gad, Asher, Issachar, Zebulun, Manasseh, and Ephraim.

The remaining two tribes (Judah and Benjamin) kept King Solomon's son, King Rehoboam, as their king and less than five years later, Egypt fought against Jerusalem and took many treasures from the temple.

Now when the Neo-Assyrian Empire came up against the two tribes in the south, they were unsuccessful because they were obedient to God. Hezekiah was the King of the two tribes, but once he died, the people become disobedient and they, too, were punished.

The Israelites understood that in Deuteronomy 28 there were blessings that they and their future generations would receive if they remained obedient to God. But, also in that same chapter, it warned them of the curses that would be bestowed upon them if they were disobedient. The Israelites were constantly disobedient to their God throughout the Bible, so again, I ask: What group of people can be identified by these curses?

In 597 BC, and because of their idolatry and disobedience to their God, Babylonian King Nebuchadnezzar II captured Jerusalem, taking thousands of them captive to Babylon.

Following the removal of the rest of the House of Judah by the Babylonians (King Nebuchadnezzar) around 586 BC, the Edomites, who had assisted the Babylonians in capturing the Judahites, moved in to occupy the land of Judah, later known as Judaea, as did many other Canaanite tribes. The book of Ezra tells us that only a tiny remnant of the House of Judah (Jerusalem) returned to Canaan following their seventy years in captivity in Babylon. They were members of the tribes of Judah, Benjamin, and Levi.

When this small group of Judahites arrived in Judaea, they found it to be a very different place from that which they had left seventy years before. The returning Judahites were initially living in fear because of all the foreign people now living in Judaea, and even lists them for us (Esau, the twin brother of Jacob-Israel, had joined himself through marriage to the Canaanites and Hittites, among others). The offspring of Esau was Edom.

They were once again conquered by Pompey's Siege (63 BC). The Roman general Pompey was in the region, fresh from his success in the Third Mithridatic War. When both sides appealed to the Romans to settle their dispute, Pompey intervened.

Herod the Great's Siege (37 BC): Roman forces helped him retake Judea, ending with the forty-day siege of Jerusalem in 37 BC. Herod's supporters and Roman troops under Marc Anthony stormed the city. The Romans went on a rampage, doing much damage to the city that their ally intended to rule. Herod later rebuilt the city.

Titus's Siege (70 AD): 66 to 73 AD saw the first of three major Jewish revolts against their Roman overlords. During the suppression of this revolt, the future Roman Emperor Titus besieged Jerusalem with four legions in 70 AD. The city was conquered and once again pillaged, the Second Temple burned down and the population of the city exiled or enslaved.

WHO ARE THE EDOMITES AND WHY ARE THEY SO IMPORTANT?

According to the Encyclopaedia Britannica, Edom was an ancient land bordering ancient Israel, in what is now southwestern Jordan, which lies between the Dead Sea and the Gulf of Aqaba. The Edomites probably occupied the area about the 13th Century BC. Though closely related to the Israelites (according to the Bible, they were descendants of Esau); they had frequent conflicts with them and were probably subject to them at the time of the Israelite kingdom (11th to 10th Century BC). Edom prospered because of its strategic location on the trade route between Arabia and the Mediterranean and its copper industry in Ezion-Geber. The Nabataeans later conquered Edom and Moab, and the Edomites migrated to southern Judaea, where they were known in New Testament times as Idumeans.

Jacob and Esau were twin brothers born to Isaac and Rebekah. Esau was born first and became the legal heir to the family birthright, which included being heir to the Covenant between God and Abraham. This birthright was a link in the line of descent through which the Promised Messiah was to come.

God knew Esau's descendants would become enemies of Israel for generations to come, and He knew Jacob was a man of integrity and He had preordained that Jacob would be in the lineage of Jesus.

To gain a better understanding of the relationship between the Israelites and the Edomites, read Genesis 25:19-34:

[19] *This is the account of the family line of Abraham's son Isaac. Abraham became the father of Isaac,* [20] *and Isaac was forty years old when he married Rebekah daughter of Bethuel the Aramean from Paddan Aram and sister of Laban the Aramean.*

[21] *Isaac prayed to the LORD on behalf of his wife, because she was childless. The LORD answered his prayer, and his wife Rebekah became pregnant.*

[22] *The babies jostled each other within her, and she said, "Why is this happening to me?" So she went to inquire of the LORD.*

[23] *The LORD said to her, "Two nations are in your womb, and two peoples from within you will be separated; one people will be stronger than the other, and the older will serve the younger."*

[24] *When the time came for her to give birth, there were twin boys in her womb.*

[25] *The first to come out was red, and his whole body was like a hairy garment; so they named him Esau.*

[26] *After this, his brother came out, with his hand grasping Esau's heel; so he was named Jacob. Isaac was sixty years old when Rebekah gave birth to them.*

[27] *The boys grew up, and Esau became a skillful hunter, a man of the open country, while Jacob was content to stay at home among the tents.*

[28] *Isaac, who had a taste for wild game, loved Esau, but Rebekah loved Jacob.*

[29] *Once when Jacob was cooking some stew, Esau came in from the open country, famished.*

[30] *He said to Jacob, "Quick, let me have some of that red stew! I'm famished!" (That is why he was also called Edom.)*

[31] *Jacob replied, "First sell me your birthright."*

[32] *"Look, I am about to die," Esau said. "What good is the birthright to me?"*

[33] *But Jacob said, "Swear to me first." So he swore an oath to him, selling his birthright to Jacob.*

[34] *Then Jacob gave Esau some bread and some lentil stew. He ate and drank, and then got up and left. So Esau despised his birthright.*

The Hebrew word Edom means "red," and the Hebrew Bible relates it to the name of its founder, Esau, the elder son of Isaac because he was born "red all over." As a young adult, he sold his birthright to his brother, Jacob, for "red pottage." The Tanakh also describes the Edomites as descendants of Esau, but Genesis 36: 9-31 tells exactly who these Edomites are:

⁹ This is the account of Esau's descendants, the Edomites, who lived in the hill country of Seir.

¹⁰ These are the names of Esau's sons: Eliphaz, the son of Esau's wife Adah; and Reuel, the son of Esau's wife Basemath.

¹¹ The descendants of Eliphaz were Teman, Omar, Zepho, Gatam, and Kenaz. 12 Timna, the concubine of Esau's son Eliphaz, gave birth to a son named Amalek. These are the descendants of Esau's wife Adah.

¹³ The descendants of Reuel were Nahath, Zerah, Shammah, and Mizzah. These are the descendants of Esau's wife Basemath.

¹⁴ Esau also had sons through Oholibamah, the daughter of Anah and granddaughter of Zibeon. Their names were Jeush, Jalam, and Korah.

¹⁵ These are the descendants of Esau who became the leaders of various clans:

The descendants of Esau's oldest son, Eliphaz, became the leaders of the clans of Teman, Omar, Zepho, Kenaz, 16 Korah, Gatam, and Amalek. These are the clan leaders in the land of Edom who descended from Eliphaz. All these were descendants of Esau's wife Adah.

¹⁷ The descendants of Esau's son Reuel became the leaders of the clans of Nahath, Zerah, Shammah, and Mizzah. These are the clan leaders in the land of Edom who descended from Reuel. All these were descendants of Esau's wife Basemath.

¹⁸ The descendants of Esau and his wife Oholibamah became the leaders of the clans of Jeush, Jalam, and Korah. These are the clan leaders who descended from Esau's wife Oholibamah, the daughter of Anah.

¹⁹ These are the clans descended from Esau (also known as Edom), identified by their clan leaders.

Original Peoples of Edom

²⁰ *These are the names of the tribes that descended from Seir the Horite. They lived in the land of Edom: Lotan, Shobal, Zibeon, Anah, 21 Dishon, Ezer, and Dishan. These were the Horite clan leaders, the descendants of Seir, who lived in the land of Edom.*

²² *The descendants of Lotan were Hori and Hemam. Lotan's sister was named Timna.*

²³ *The descendants of Shobal were Alvan, Manahath, Ebal, Shepho, and Onam.*

²⁴ *The descendants of Zibeon were Aiah and Anah. (This is the Anah who discovered the hot springs in the wilderness while he was grazing his father's donkeys.)*

²⁵ *The descendants of Anah were his son, Dishon, and his daughter, Oholibamah.*

²⁶ *The descendants of Dishon were Hemdan, Eshban, Ithran, and Keran.*

²⁷ *The descendants of Ezer were Bilhan, Zaavan, and Akan.*

²⁸ *The descendants of Dishan were Uz and Aran.*

²⁹ *So these were the leaders of the Horite clans: Lotan, Shobal, Zibeon, Anah, 30 Dishon, Ezer, and Dishan. The Horite clans are named after their clan leaders, who lived in the land of Seir.*

³¹ *These are the kings who ruled in the land of Edom before any king ruled over the Israelites.*

Esau's grandson, Zepho, who was the son of Eliphaz, has a very interesting story. There came a time when Jacob died and his sons went to bury him in Hebron, in the cave of Machpelah. This was where their parents, Isaac and Rebekah, were buried so of course, Esau wasn't going to allow this to happen without a fight therefore a battle ensued. Esau and his sons rose against the sons of Jacob along with the Egyptian people. During that battle, Esau was killed which caused the sons of Esau to wage war against the sons of Jacob. The sons of Esau were defeated and Zepho was taken captive along with about fifty of his men. Zepho would later escape from his prison in Egypt after Joseph died, and fled to Africa. There King Angeas (a descendant of Ham) of the Carthaginian Empire located on the North Coast of Africa welcomed Zepho. He had been a friend to the Edomites in the past and King Angeas was honored to have Zepho there because he knew he was a great warrior and made Zepho the captain of his host. During his time there, Zepho was constantly trying to get King Angeas to go to war with the sons of Jacob and the Egyptians to avenge the death of his brethren and his grandfather, Esau. The king knew the power of the sons of Jacob and what they did to the sons of Esau and refused to go to war with them, but Zepho was persistent and continued to entice the king daily, trying to get him to go to war with the sons of Jacob. Finally, the king agreed to go to war with the sons of Jacob but first, he wanted to consult with a young servant by the name of Balaam. (Balaam is spoken of in Numbers 22 when he was summoned to try to curse the Israelites.) Balaam was only fifteen years old at the time and very wise. He had a very good understanding of the art of witchcraft. King Angeas asked Balaam to use his witchcraft to see if they would prevail in the battle if they attacked the sons of Jacob. Balaam informed the king that he would not prevail if he went to war, and it was decided he would not go to war with Israel. Upon hearing that King Angeas was not going to attack the sons of Jacob, Zepho fled Africa and went into Chittim (Kittiym) where he was received with great honor.

For years before Zepho went to Chittim, King Angeas would go into Chittim whenever he wanted and would plunder them and take whatever he wanted. There came a time after Zepho had gotten there at the revolution of the year and King Angeas came to plunder Chittim as usual, but this time it was different. Zepho was now in Chittim. When he heard of this, he gave orders to fight them. Zepho defeated them. The people of Chittim saw his valor and made him their king. Zepho also made war with Tubal and the Islands. So now, Zepho is the king of Italia and Chittim where he ruled for fifty years. King Angeas and his brother would go up against Zepho and would be defeated so severely that King Angeas would fear Zepho for the rest of his life. The youngest son of King Angeas would later become king and be considered one of the greatest generals in history. He would march an army of war elephants over the Pyrenees mountains and the Alps mountains into Italy and defeated the largest army Rome had ever put together. In the Apocrypha, his name is spelled Annible, but he was known to most of us in history as Hannible (of Carthage) the Great.

According to the Zondervan's Bible Dictionary, Chittim, Kittim, descendants of Javan; it not only applies to Cyprus but also the Islands and the coasts of the Mediterranean.

Javan is through the lineage of Noah's son, Japheth.

The land of Italia is the territory on which the city of Rome resides.

According to Easton's Bible dictionary, Tubal"

1. 1. The fifth son of Japheth (Genesis 10:2).

2. 2. A nation, probably descended from the son of Japheth. It is mentioned by Isaiah (66:19), along with Javan, and by Ezekiel (27:13), along with Meshech, among the traders with Tyre, also among the confederates of Gog (Ezekiel 38:2, 3; 39:1), and with Meshech among the nations which were to be destroyed (32:26). This nation was probably the Tiberini of the Greek historian Herodotus, a people of the Asiatic highland west of the Upper Euphrates, the southern range of the Caucasus, on the east of the Black Sea. We have Zepho, the grandson of Esau that is now the King of Italia and Chittim.

2 Chronicles 20:10-13 tells of Jehoshaphat, who was King of the two-tribe kingdom of Israel at the same time King A'hab and Jezebel ruled the northern tribes. There came a time when the countries of Mo'ab, Am'mon and Edom were coming to attack them. With God's intervention, the invaders eventually turned against one another, thus failing in their plan. Edom also revolted in the time of King Jehoram of Judah and elected a king of its own (2 Kings 8:20-22; 2 Chronicles. 21:8). The writer of the book of Kings reports that "To this day Edom has been in rebellion against Judah." Jehoram's son, Amaziah, attacked and defeated the Edomites, seizing Selah (2 Kings 14:7; 2 Chron. 25:11-1), the kingdom.

THE ISRAELITES

Esau was going to kill his brother, Jacob, because he stole his birthright, but he was going to wait until their father, Isaac, died. Once Rebecca learned of this, she insisted Jacob leave, and even though he at first resisted, he eventually went to Mesopotamia to live with Laban, the son of Bethuel, who was the brother of Rebecca. Jacob ended up serving in the house of Leban for twenty years. There came a time when Jacob, his two wives, his maidservants, and his eleven sons crossed the ford of the Jabbok. He sent them across first, leaving him all alone. This was when he wrestled a man until daybreak. When the man realized he could not overpower Jacob, he touched him on his hip, causing it to be wrenched. It was this encounter that made Jacob known as Israel because "you have struggled with God and with humans and have overcome."

Jacob had twelve sons known today as the twelve tribes of Israel and even though all the nations around Israel had kings, Israel did not have a king, but they wanted to be like the other nations so they asked God to give them a king. Three kings ruled over the twelve tribes of Israel, each for forty years before dividing into northern and southern kingdoms—one with ten tribes and one with only two. King Saul was the first king of Israel. He came from a wealthy family and was a handsome man, but that was not why God had chosen him to be king. God chose him because he was humble.

King David was the second king of Israel, and I believe almost everyone remembers the story of David and Goliath, but most don't know that David eventually became the King of Israel.

King Solomon was the last king of the twelve tribes of Israel. King Solomon not only had more wisdom than anyone that had ever lived, but he also had the blessings of both riches and glory and even he became disobedient to God. He was the last king of the twelve tribes before dividing into the northern and southern kingdoms.

King Solomon built the First Temple in 1000 BC after King David conquered Jerusalem and made it his capital. Nebuchadnezzar, the King of Babylon, destroyed the Temple in 586 BC when he conquered Jerusalem. The Edomites attacked Israel under Saul's rulership. King David would later defeat the rogue nation, annexing their land. At the fall of the First Temple, the Edomites attacked Judah and looted the Temple along with the Babylonians, accelerating its destruction. John Hyrcanus forced the Edomites to convert to Judaism, and then they became an active part of the Jewish people. A famous Edomites was Herod, who built the Second Temple.

Encyclopedia.com says, "Hyrcanus achieved the complete independence of Judea and undertook extensive conquests throughout the whole of the land of Israel. At first, he turned to the center of the country, seizing Shechem and destroying the Samaritan temple on Mt. Gerizim. Later he conquered Idumea (Edom) and compelled its inhabitants to adopt Judaism. From this time the Idumeans became an inseparable part of the Hebrew people."

This forced conversion of the Edomites to Judaism was a disastrous decision for the House of Judah because, after a period, history seemed to have forgotten that there were two different Israelites in Jerusalem. There were the ones that were Hebrews through their lineage and the others that were converted Edomites.

So now living in Jerusalem, according to The War Of The Jews by Flavius Josephus, "For there are three philosophical sects among the Jews. The followers of the first of which are the Pharisees; of the second, the Sadducees; and the third sect... are called Essenes. These last are Jews [properly "of Judah"] by birth, and seem to have a greater affection for one another than the other sects have."

In John 8:31-33, Jesus was having a conversation with the Jewish religious leaders.

31 Then said Jesus to those Jews which believed on him, If ye continue in my word, then are ye my disciples indeed;

32 And ye shall know the truth, and the truth shall make you free.

33 They answered him, We be Abraham's seed, and were never in bondage to any man: how sayest thou, Ye shall be made free?

Understand this, the Israelites, by birth, had been in bondage before—in Egypt, the Assyrians, and by the Babylonians. The Edomites were actually from the lineage of Abraham but through his son, Esau, not Jacob-Israel. So these religious leaders that Jesus was talking to were more than likely Edomites.

Romans 9:7-8 says, *⁷ Being descendants of Abraham doesn't make them truly Abraham's children. For the Scriptures say, "Isaac is the son through whom your descendants will be counted," though Abraham had other children, too. ⁸ This means that Abraham's physical descendants are not necessarily children of God. Only the children of the promise are considered Abraham's children.*

According to the Jewish virtual library, traditional enemies of the Israelites, the Edomites, were the descendants of Esau who often battled the Jewish nation. Edom was in southeast Palestine, stretched from the Red Sea at Elath to the Dead Sea, and encompassed some of Israel's most fertile land. The Edomites attacked Israel under Saul's rulership. King David would later defeat the rogue nation, annexing their land. At the fall of the First Temple, the Edomites attacked Judah and looted the Temple, accelerating its destruction. John Hyrcanus then forced the Edomites to convert to Judaism, and they became an active part of the Jewish people. Eventually, over time, it was difficult to distinguish the difference between the converted Jews and the Jews came were born through the lineage of Isaac and Jacob. through true lineage. So surely the converted Edomite Jews rose to power politicly as well as religiously. Famous Edomites include king Herod, who built the Second Temple.

The Jewish library also quoted that Julius Caesar appointed a governor to keep watch over the country, the son of an Idumean (Edomite) who was forced to convert to Judaism, a man as mentioned before by the name of Herod.

This is confirmation that not only did the Edomites become part of the Jewish community religiously, they also became a very powerful part of the community politically.

This helps with understanding why so many of the Jewish religious leaders did not accept Jesus (and to this very day anticipate the arrival of the first coming of Jesus) because they were not from the tribe of Judah or any of the twelve tribes. Though they were the lineage of Abraham, they were the offspring of Esau, Edomites, only converted to practice Judaism.

Edom first established their kingdom in the southern area of modern-day Jordan and later migrated into the southern parts of the Kingdom of Judah when Judah was first weakened and then destroyed by the Babylonians in the 6th Century BC. The Kingdom of Edom was large and bordered the Kingdom of Judea, and eventually, the Edomites migrated as far south into Judea as Hebron. Ironically, Judas Iscariot was the only apostle whom the Bible (potentially) identifies by his town of origin. Some scholars have linked his surname "Iscariot," to Queriot (or Kerioth), a small town a few miles south of Hebron. So Judas (Iscariot) is not a last name, but a geographical location. Queriot was an Edomite city, so could it be possible that this was a clue that was left for us that Judas Iscariot was an Edomite?

On the next page, is a map of ancient Judah and Edom.

Jesus was talking to the Pharisees in John 8:32-33: (32) "Then you will know the truth, and the truth will set you free. (33)We are offspring of Abraham and have never been enslaved to anyone. How is it that you say, 'You will become free'?" The Pharisees were not lying to Jesus. Esau was the son of Isaac, which made Abraham his grandfather.

The Siege of Jerusalem in the year 70 CE was the decisive event of the First Jewish–Roman War, in which the Roman army captured the city of Jerusalem and destroyed both the city and its Temple. According to the Bible, before this siege, God had warned the Jews to flee the city because the Romans would destroy it. Some of them obeyed and left the city. After the Romans conquered Jerusalem, the Romans sold some of the Jews as slaves or transported them as captives after the fall of Judea. Others joined the existing diaspora, while others remained in Judea. The Jews in the diaspora were accepted into the Roman

Empire, but with the rise of Christianity, restrictions grew. Forced expulsions and persecution resulted in substantial shifts in the international centers of Jewish life. Judea expelled Jewish communities, sending them to various Roman provinces in the Middle East, Europe, and North Africa.

In the past, each time its enemies conquered the Israelites, the ones that were not taken away as slaves and able to escape usually fled to Egypt and North Africa. But this time was different because converted Jews and those that were from the lineage of Abraham through Isaac living in Jerusalem fled the city to hide. To a place where they can blend in with the people that look like them. Some fled to Europe and others to north Africa. The Israelites often fled to a place where they could blend in with people that looked like them.

Deuteronomy 28 says, *"God's people will be taken away from the land that they possess never to return."* Are there no Jews living in Israel today? So who are those who call themselves Jews that occupy Israel today? Most of the Jews that occupy Israel today are Khazars. Khazar was a country in the northern Caucasus region and was part of the western Turkic empire (in Turkistan). You may ask: How do we know they are not from one of the twelve tribes of Israel? Or that lost tribe, which they are often referred? Arthur Koestler wrote in his book, *The Thirteenth Tribe*, "The large majority of surviving Jews in the world is of Eastern European—and thus mainly Khazar—origin. If so, this would mean that their ancestors came not from the Jordan but from the Volga, not from Canaan but from the Caucasus, once believed to be the cradle of the Aryan race; and that genetically they are more closely related to the Hun, Uigur and the Magyar tribes than to the seed of Abraham, Isaac, and Jacob." Again, let us take a trip back in history so we can see where these people originated and how they came to call themselves Jews.

For this, we will go back to the Bible in Genesis and look at the Table of Nations, but this time we will look at Noah's son, Japeth.

Genesis 10 is the account of Shem, Ham, and Japheth, Noah's sons, who had sons after the flood.

The Japhethites

2 The sons[a] of Japheth:

Gomer, Magog, Madai, Javan, Tubal, Meshek and Tiras.

3 The sons of Gomer:

Ashkenaz, Riphath, and Togarmah.

We can trace the Khazars can back to Kozar, a son of Togarmah. Togarmah was a son of Gomer, of the family of Japheth, and brother of Ashkenaz and Riphath. (Genesis 10:3) His descendants became a people engaged in agriculture, breeding horses and mules to be sold in Tyre. (Ezek. 27:14; 38:6) They were also a military people and were well skilled in using arms. Ezekiel 27:14 mentions Togarmah after Tubal, Javan, and Mesech as supplying horses and mules to the Tyrians, and in 38:6 it is said to have supplied soldiers to the army of Gog.

Armenian Moses of Chorene and Georgian Leonti Mroveli regarded Togarmah as the founder of their nations, along with other Caucasian people.

According to Moses of Chorene's History of Armenia and Leonti Mroveli's medieval Georgian Chronicles, "Thargamos" was thought to have lived in Babylon, before he received the "land between two Seas and two Mountains" (i.e. the Caucasus) in his possession. He then settled near Mount Ararat and divided his land among his sons, one being Kovar whose people became known as Khazarians. The Khazar ruler Joseph ben Aaron writes in his letters: "You ask us also in your epistle: "Of what people, of what family, and of what tribe are you? Know that we are descendants of Japhet, through his son, Togarmah. I have found in the genealogical books of my ancestors that Togarmah had ten sons."

According to encyclopedia.com, "Around the middle of the 8th Century, the king of the Khazars and many of the Khazar nobility accepted the Jewish faith. According to a widespread legend, the conversion of the Khazars to Judaism followed a religious discussion in which their king was particularly impressed by the arguments of Jewish theologians.

After the conversion of the leading Khazars to Judaism, many Jews, including several Jewish scholars, migrated to the Khazar kingdom, where they kept in touch with the intellectual centers of the Jewish world, especially those in Mesopotamia and Palestine. The literary sources show explicitly that the Khazars acknowledged the authority of the Talmud; hence, they must not have been affected in religious matters by the Karaites.

The Khazars' acceptance of Judaism coincided with a period of peaceful development in their history when they focused their attention on the strengthening of their power at home and the extending of their political influence abroad. They thus established new commercial centers of importance at various places throughout their sphere of influence, and in these places, as well as in their older cities, such as Itil in the delta of the Volga, and Samkarsh and Tamatarcha on the Bosphorus, the Jewish element formed an important part of the population. At Semender on the Caspian Sea, a ruler of the Khazars, who was likewise a convert to Judaism, had his headquarters. Although the most important posts among the Khazars were held by families which had converted to Judaism, and there reigned in Khazaria, a spirit of religious toleration such as was rarely to be found at the time in Christian or Moslem countries.

In an article published on the World Zionist Organization's (WZO) website:

> "REMARKABLY, the Khazars, a people of Turkic origin, converted to the Jewish religion in the 9th century, beginning with the royal house and spreading gradually among the general populace. Judaism is now known to have been more widespread among the Khazar inhabitants of the Khazar kingdom than previously thought. In 1999, Russian archaeologists announced they had successfully reconstructed a Khazarian vessel from the Don River region, revealing four inscriptions of the word "Israel" in Hebrew lettering. It is now the accepted opinion among most scholars in the field that the conversion of the Khazars to Judaism was widespread, and not limited merely to the royal house and nobility. Ibn al-Faqih wrote, "All of the Khazars are Jews." Christian of Stavelot wrote in 864 that "all of them profess the Jewish faith in its entirety."

WHAT HAPPENED TO THE KHAZAR PEOPLE?

There was a Russian attack in 965 CE, which was aimed at the Khazar capital. Some of Khazars eventually were absorbed into the Russian society while others disappeared into different countries in Europe (where they eventually flourished) one of which is Germany.

"Ashkenazi" refers to Jewish settlers who established communities along the Rhine River in Western Germany and Northern France dating to the Middle Ages. The name Ashkenazi derives from the biblical figure of Ashkenaz, the first son of Gomer. Ashkenaz was the brother of Kozar (Khazar). So are these Ashkenazi Jewish settlers the offspring of the biblical figure Ashkenaz? It appears that we have two of the offspring of Japath that have converted to Judaism living in Germany and eventually the Ashkenazi had settlements all over the world.

During the tenth century in Germany and France, the Ashkenazis were economic pioneers and had many trading connections with the Mediterranean and the East. In France, they owned vineyards and made wine. By the end of the eleventh century, anti-Semitism started to grow. In the twelfth and thirteenth centuries, many of them became moneylenders. The countries benefited from the taxes they were forced to pay but eventually, they were expelled from France. In Germany, they were forced to live in Ghettos away from the rest of society and by 1750, the majority of the Jews in the American Colonies were Ashkenazi.

In the fifteenth century, the Roman Catholic Church divided the world in half, granting Portugal a monopoly on trade in West Africa. Pope Nicholas V buoyed Portuguese efforts and issued the Romanus Pontifex of 1455, which affirmed Portugal's exclusive rights to territories it claimed along the West African coast and the trade from those areas. It granted the right to invade, plunder and "reduce their persons to perpetual slavery."

In his book, *The Secret Relationship Between Blacks and Jews*, Minister Louis Farrakhan states, that in 1460, the Jews were the masters of the nautical sciences in Portugal, and also how that nation was importing seven to eight hundred slaves yearly. Minister Farrakhan also states it not only lists the Jewish owned slave ships but also the names of the families that owned the ships. They even list the census records with each Jewish family, the state and city that they resided in as well as how many slaves that they owned.

It appears that just as it happened in Jerusalem during the days of John Hyrcanus, the converted Jews became very powerful not only economically but politically as well, and most didn't and still don't even realize that you had converted Jews and Israelites through lineage (bloodline) still in the world today only most of the Israelites through their lineage don't even know who they are.

At the turn of the 20th century, European Jews were migrating to Palestine in large numbers because of religious persecution. In Russia, Jewish people were segregated and in 1881 Russians began the mass killings of Jews. The Jews that migrated to Palestine came mostly from Europe and Russia. (Remember the Khazars that had not fled to Germany and other European countries hundreds of years earlier had just become a part of the Russian empire) During the holocaust in World war II, many Jews illegally entered Palestine and on November 29, 1947, the UN General Assembly voted on the partition plan, adopted by 33 votes to 13 with 10 abstentions. In summary, The Israeli-Palestinian conflict dates back to the end of the nineteenth century and this Partition Plan divided the British Mandate of Palestine into Arab and Jewish states. On May 14, 1948, the State of Israel was created, sparking the first Arab-Israeli War. The war ended with an Israeli victory, but seven hundred fifty thousand Palestinians were displaced and the territory was divided into three parts: the State of Israel, the West Bank (of the Jordan River), and the Gaza Strip. This is the reason for the constant conflicts, wars, in that part of the world. For thousands of years the Israelites have been fighting wars for their "promised land" but what does the Bible say about Jerusalem today?

Luke 21:24 says, *"And they shall fall by the edge of the sword, and shall be led away captive into all nations: and Jerusalem shall be trodden down of the Gentiles until the times of the Gentiles be fulfilled."* Gentile is defined as a person who is not Jewish.

These are not my words but the words of Luke the Physician He was not one of the original twelve Apostles but could have possibly been one of the seventy disciples appointed by Jesus. Everything that you have read I urge you to do your own research and come to your own conclusion.

CONNECTING THE DOTS

*A*braham was a descendant of Noah's son Shem and was from Ur of the Chaldees in Mesopotamia. Ur was the center of Sumerian culture. The Sumerian people referred to themselves as "The Blacks-headed people."

Exodus 4:11 tells us that Moses was given a powerful sign from God when he was told by God to put his hand in his cloak and when he took it out and it was white as snow. He placed it back inside his cloak and took it out it was restored like the rest of his flesh. This is interesting because if he was already white what great sign would it be if his hand turned white and back white?

We know that Moses was raised in the house of the Pharaoh of Egypt as an Egyptian and we also know that the Egyptians, as well as the Africans (Libyans), were the descendants of Ham, and Ham is said to be the progenitor of the Blacks races but not the Negro. So if Moses had been living as an Egyptian then he had to have had the same skin color as them. Even when we read in the Bible about Jacob's son, Joseph, who was sold into slavery by his brothers in Egypt. Years later, Joseph ended up being a powerful man in Egypt when there was a famine in the land and Joseph's brothers went to Egypt for food and did not recognize their own brother. They thought that he was an Egyptian. It wasn't until they went back a second time and brought their youngest brother that Joseph revealed to them who he was.

There are many examples in the Bible and even in history outside of the Bible that identify God's true people. This history has been hidden and even stolen from us so that we would not know who we are. Throughout the Bible, Edom has always been an enemy of the Israelites. Why would we not think for a second today that it has changed? Just like the days of Jesus when the converted Jews who were mostly Edomites rose to power and eventually became the religious leaders in Jerusalem.

Was it only by coincidence that Blacks were not taken from all over Africa but mostly from one part of the continent?

In the year 1484 King John of Portugal deported an estimated tens of thousands of Blacks Jews to the African Island of San Thome which is near Nigeria because they would not accept baptism into Christianity. Pope Nicolas V issued a series of papal bulls that granted Portugal the right to enslave sub-Saharan Africans. Don't believe for a minute that these people didn't know who or what people that they were enslaving.

In Joshua 15:42, the cities of Judah are named and one of the sixteen cities is called Ashan. Ashan is in Joshua 19:7, speaking of the inheritance of the clans of the tribe of Simeon. There was an empire in what is now Ghana called the Ashanti Empire, which comprised of Black Hebrews. In his book, *The Negro Question,* Lee Cummings says, "It has been recorded that the Ashanti or Korromante were so rebellious that the Spanish and French would not permit them into their colonies and that there was only one market open to them and that market was the British colonies."

There is example after example of slave ships coming to this land with Blacks from Judea. Many people (including me before my research) have never heard of Negroland and have never even given a second thought as to the origin of the word Negro. My mother's birth certificate has her nationality as Negro. Over the years, the nationality has changed from Negro to Colored to Black and now African American. This is all to keep you in the dark as to who you really are; if you truly understood how powerful you are and your connection to the Creator, you would move a lot differently.

I cannot encourage enough the importance of reading. There is a reason we can endure so much. Why is it that we are hated by the same people whose ancestors not only bought and sold our ancestors, but also raped, tortured, and treated them like animals? The answer:

We are God's chosen people and as it reads in the Bible, "I know thy works, and tribulation, and poverty, (but thou art rich) and I know the blasphemy of them which say they are Jews, and are not, but are the synagogue of Satan."

So, who is Edom? The answer is right in front of us. Noah had three sons: Japheth, Ham, and Shem. His sons were given a lot of land, according to the Table of Nations in Genesis 10. It is believed that Caucasians come from Japheth, which is far from the truth. We have been taught this lie to further hide the truth—the descendants of Ham, Japheth, and Shem were all Black. This all changed with the birth of Esau and Jacob. Esau, who is Edom, is described in the scriptures as the Red people who later described themselves as White. Jules Michelet, a French historian born in 1798 AD, wrote that the Athenians described the Romans as having a fierce face with red hair, green eyes, and a red complexion spotted with white. They thought the Romans looked amusing and found their physical characteristics strange because of their red appearance. Jeremiah 49:10 says, *"That I have made Esau bare, I have uncovered his secret places, and he shall not be able to hide himself: his seed is spoiled, and his brethren, and his neighbors, and he is not."* Edom has strategically mixed his seed throughout the planet with the other gentile nations, which basically means he has whited out these other nations. Dr. Beneyah Yashar'el wrote, "Esau was different and came out red though he was the product of Black parents." Also, "Esau, the first red man, now described as a white man mixed with the Black gentile nations and produced a mixed race of people described as white because of the color of their skin and Esau's phenotype." Remember that Zepho was the grandson of Esau and was made king of Chittim (Kittiym) which is Rome. Soon after, descendants of Esau followed Zepho into the land that was occupied by the descendants of Japheth. They spread throughout Italy, Greece, and Europe. Dr. Beneyah Yashar'el also wrote, "History shows that since the Empire of Edom-Rome ruled the earth for the past two-thousand years, they were able to enlarge and replace the descendants of Japheth. But scripture also shows the names of the sons of Japheth and the sons of Edom differed. The Edomites replaced the names of the sons of Japheth through marriage and conquest." Genesis 9:27 reads, *"May God enlarge Japheth, and let him dwell in the tents of Shem, and let Canaan be his servant."* We must not forget that Esau (Edom) is an offspring of Shem therefore he and his offspring are Semitic. Though they are descendants of Abraham but not of Jacob therefore they are not Israelites.

Again, I urge you to study and do your research—the information is out there. This is a time of enlightenment, my people, and it is up to you to learn this information so you can teach others.

HITLER'S
Confessions

ARMINE
KNOT
NANCE

Hitler said even in his death he will start World War 3. One of his soliders asked how? Hitler replied, "The day mankind finds out what I was trying to defend this nation, Germany, from then thats the day World War 3 will start. For on that day, mankind will learn that I was trying to save my Nation from The Free Masons, the Illuminati, the jews. For if the Americans wins the war, then they will conquer the world and forever be a slave to the jews and they will try to conquer God. *Do you know who America has in its posession?* "NO," the solider replied. *The Americans has the jewels of God. The Americans have stolen God's precious jewels.* "What do you mean his precious jewels?" THE SOLIDER asked. Hitler said, *"America has stolen the jews. The Jews of God. His jewelry. The Negros. They are the True Hebrews.*

ABOUT THE AUTHOR

Michael Timmons is a native of Washington, DC, and was raised by his mother and three older sisters. Seeking a better life for her children, his mother moved the family to Prince George's County, Maryland. Being an avid reader, his mother passed this trait down to Michael, who took a real passion for reading Greek mythology at a young age. When he was a teenager, his mother became a Jehovah's Witness, so he spent a lot of time at the Kingdom Hall and reading the Bible. Once Michael turned sixteen, his mother allowed him to make his own choice regarding his religion. "Make the truth your own," was the motto his mother constantly preached, so he felt the only way to make the truth his own was to learn everything he could about other religions.

At the time, he didn't know his spiritual journey would take him around the world, searching for a truth that would teach him that once we look outside of the box, or our own personal truths, we will see that most people are seeking the same truth—to make sense of this world we live in, to live better lives, and a hope for a better future.

CPSIA information can be obtained
at www.ICGtesting.com
Printed in the USA
BVHW021006100621
609275BV00008B/1756